SNAP SHOT™

Senior Editor
Mary Ling

Art Editor
Joanna Pocock

Editor
Finbar Hawkins

Designers
Claire Penny, Jane Thomas

Production
Catherine Semark

Consultant
Philip Wilkinson

US Editor
Camela Decaire

A SNAPSHOT™ BOOK

SNAPSHOT™ is an imprint of Covent Garden Books
95 Madison Avenue
New York, NY 10016

Copyright © 1995 Covent Garden Books Ltd., London.
2 4 6 8 10 9 7 5 3 1

Photography by Geoff Brightling, Mike Dunning, Richard Hill,
Colin Keates, Dave King, Bob Langrish, Karl Shone, Steve Shott,
Kate Warren, Jerry Young

Picture credits: Bruce Coleman Ltd/Jeff Foott Productions:
8/9b/Steve Kaufman: 17t/Wayne Lankinen: 16t and
17b/Leonard Lee Rue: 16b; C M Dixon: 14bl;
Robert Harding Picture Library: 9tr, 15b/Robert Cundy: 9c;
Wychwood Dynascha owned by Mrs G Harwood: 28tl;
Werner Forman Archive: 30; Zefa: Maroon 6/7b/Kummels:
20b/Corneel Voigt: 10b.
Clay sculpture of a traditional bear fetish by
Tony Da, San Ildefonso Pueblo, photographed by
Larry Phillips for Institute of American Indian
Arts Museum (SILD-23): 14c

Special thanks to Richard Hill at the
Smithsonian Institute and Simon Brascoupé

ISBN 1-56458-957-9

Every effort has been made to
trace the copyright holders and we
apologize in advance for any unintentional omissions.
We would be pleased to insert the appropriate acknowledgment
in any subsequent edition of this publication.

Color reproduction by Colourscan
Printed and bound in Belgium by Proost

INCREDIBLE

Written by
Caroline Bingham

WILD WEST

Contents

Gold

Water bottle

Quiver
and arrows

The Wild West

Think "Wild West" and what do you see? Cowboys trailing herds of cattle, American Indians riding bareback ...

Giddyup

Horses were brought to America by the Spanish in the 1500s. They made a big difference in how far and how fast people traveled.

Yee-haw!

Cowboys rode the Great Plains from the 1860s to the 1880s, driving huge cattle herds north. Sounds fun? A cowboy's life was tough and often boring.

rom Crow to Sioux, thousands of tribes lived in America.

A losing battle

Native Americans
lived in tribes. Some
tribes lived off the land
by hunting, others farmed.
The tribes tried to fight
European settlers to maintain
their way of life, but they lost
more and more territory.

*This Indian belt is made from wampum,
beads of polished shells. Wampum was
used as money and for pledges to
seal important treaties.*

A way of life

A fast drumming of hooves fills the air, while people yell and bows are drawn. The hunt is on!

Indian tribes honored animals with special dances.

After the 1860s,

Hunting to live

Before the arrival of guns and horses, Native Americans hunted buffalo with bows and arrows. Sometimes a stampede ran off the top of a cliff, and the carcasses were collected at the bottom.

Bow

Nothing wasted

The whole buffalo was used. The meat was dried, the hides made into clothes and tepees, and the horns and bones made into tools. In winter, children even played on sleds made from buffalo ribs.

Arrows were carried in a quiver.

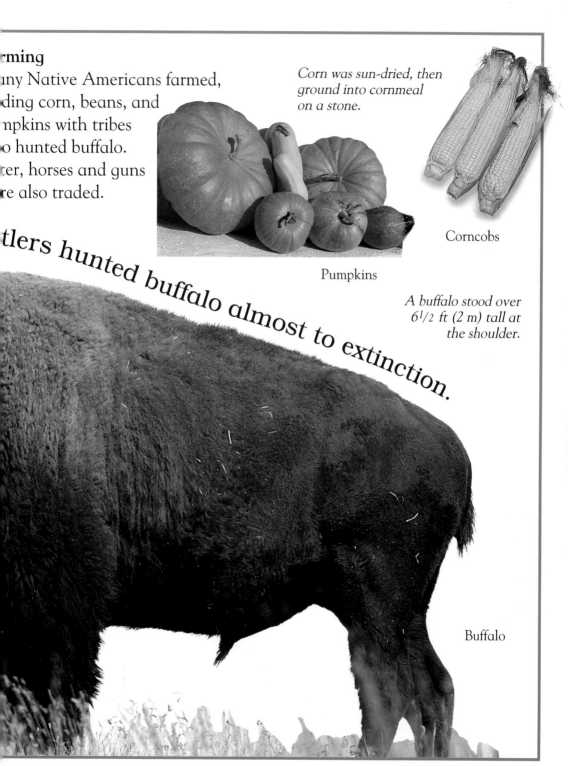

rming
ıny Native Americans farmed,
ding corn, beans, and
npkins with tribes
o hunted buffalo.
ter, horses and guns
re also traded.

Corn was sun-dried, then ground into cornmeal on a stone.

Corncobs

Pumpkins

tlers hunted buffalo almost to extinction.

A buffalo stood over 6½ ft (2 m) tall at the shoulder.

Buffalo

Tepee time!

Stretch eight or ten buffalo skins over long pole supports, and you have made a secure home – a tepee fit for a family.

Some tepees used 20 buffalo hides.

A mobile home
When a tribe moved on, two poles were strapped to a horse, forming a stretcher called a travois to carry belongings.

Painted symbols were thought to protect against illness and bad luck.

Vacation hom
Tepees provided some tribes wi
temporary summer homes
they left their villag
to follow buffa
herc

Wrapped with love

When a girl liked a boy, they would talk at a tepee's entrance, wrapped for warmth in a single blanket made from a hide.

Home sweet home

All possessions were stored inside a tepee, from clothes and headdresses to pots and pans. Rugs were scattered on the floor to provide a cozy welcome. There was even a central fireplace.

Crow Indians hand-painted this blanket.

An inner lining kept heat in and drafts out.

Tepee poles

Early learning

Life was tough on the Great Plains – Indian children had to learn fast.

Comanche Indians learned

All strapped up
Tiny babies were kept safe in cradleboards. Two prongs stuck into the ground if the carrier was accidentally dropped.

Dolls' faces were often left blank so the corn's spirit could appear.

Pinto ponies were popular because of th distinctive white and chestnut patterning.

Time for toys
Children played with toy tepees and dolls made from corn. Have you ever played with a dollhouse?

There were no classrooms. As soon as children were old enough, they were expected to join in the daily work of the tribe.

...ow to capture and tame wild horses.

Pinto pony

Toddlers on horseback

Riding was a way of life, and children were expected to begin to ride as soon as they could walk. This early start made for skilled riders.

...ome riders could ...rop down on one ...de of a horse as ...galloped and ...oot at a target ...om beneath ...s neck.

Horse art
The horse's image often decorated clothes and tepees.

Tunic

Tribal fashion

Even though different tribes spoke separate languages, they all had things in common.

Saddle

Hand signals were the simplest means of communication between tribes.

The spirit of a bear

A fetish is like a lucky charm. Indians believed that spirits were imprisoned inside certain objects, such as a bone, a feather, or a carved stick. A fetish was worn, or hidden in a tepee, so that its spirit would protect its owner.

A sacred pipe

A decorated pipe like this was very special indeed. It was smoked before a battle or as part of a peacemaking ceremony.

Bear fetish

Some sacred

A sign of braver

Tribe leaders wor colorful headdresses t show their importance A brave warrior's headdres could be so full of feathers it wo as long as the warrior was tal

How many?

Tepee

Horse

An eagle's feather was a mark of honor among all tribes.

...pes were 5 ft (1.5 m) long!

Wild West wildlife

From hefty buffalo to high-flying eagles, America teemed with wildlife. Most was hunted for food and clothing.

Jackrabbits had to be alert for both the arrow and the shotgun.

The animals and plants of the Great Plains

Antelope horns were used for headdresses.

A fast getaway
The pronghorn antelope runs almost 55 mph (about 90 kph) and has excellent sight and hearing. Native Americans used its skin to make leggings, tunics, skirts, and dresses.

Eagle power!

Native Americans saw the eagle as
a symbol of power. Birds were
important in their religion,
and many tribes believed
that birds were spirits
of the dead.

*The bald eagle
became the US's
national emblem
in 1782.*

*The bald eagle is so
named because its white
head feathers contrast
with those on its body.
It looks bald!*

provided for Native Americans and pioneers.

Prairie
chicken

Cluck, cluck

Cowboys were tied to their herd and
were rarely able to spare time to hunt.
But if a cowboy on the trail shot a
prairie chicken, it was soon added to
the pot. It made a welcome change
from the usual bacon and beans.

Pushing west

By the 1850s, thousands of people had trekke for months along the treacherous Oregon Trail, traveling across the Rocky Mountains and along the Snake River into Idaho.

Covers were made from canvas and waterproofed with paint or linseed oil.

The search for land
Pioneer families carried all their belongings in covered wagons. The journey was long and hard – pioneers faced cold weather, illness, bad food, and harsh terrain.

Two horses are pulling this wagon. Most of the pioneer wagons were pulled by oxen or mules.

Some pioneers were looking for land …

eer trails were often marked with broken
els, discarded furniture, and animal skulls.

others were lured by news of a gold rush.

Skull of a
longhorn cow

The longhorn cow was the most common cow in America until the 1880s.

Go for gold!
In 1849 more than 80,000 people flooded west, hoping to make their fortunes. Few succeeded, but they did create instant, and often lawless, towns.

Dodge City

Welcome to the "Cowboy Capital of the World" and the "Wickedest Little City in the West."

Hereford cows were brought to America from Britain in the 1880s.

New towns sprang up

Parts of the origin Dodge City have be restored for tourists to visit.

Gunfights and gambling

Dodge City lay on a spot where the railroad crossed a cattle trail, making it a dangerous place full of gunmen, gamblers, and cowboys.

at river crossings and next to railroads.

Spending spree

After three months or more on the trail, cowboys were keen to spend their money. Each town had a saloon and hotel, a bank, a blacksmith, and a general store.

Chips

Cards

Gambling was rife in the new towns.

Your shopping's in the mail

Catalog shopping made life easier for people living in remote towns or ranches. A wide selection was available – just look at this page from an old catalog.

Good guys and bad guys

A sheriff is on the trail of a fierce gunfighter.
Take cover! There's going to be a shoot-out!

Film fantasy

Although guns were carried, gunfights were not as common
as films have made it seem. But there were some notorious
outlaws, like the ruthless Billy the Kid and Emmett Dalton.

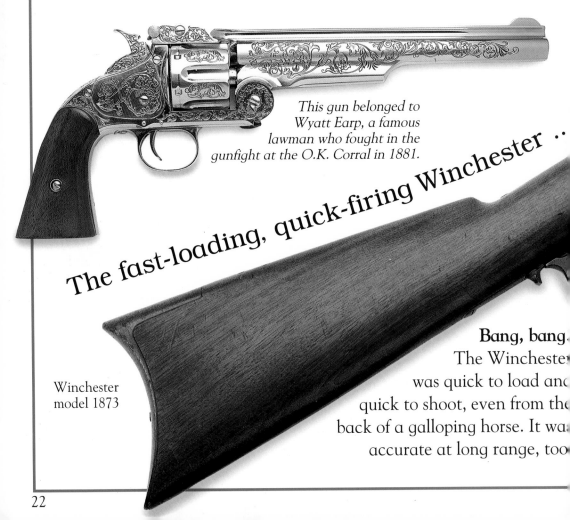

*This gun belonged to
Wyatt Earp, a famous
lawman who fought in the
gunfight at the O.K. Corral in 1881.*

The fast-loading, quick-firing Winchester ..

Winchester
model 1873

Bang, bang.
The Wincheste
was quick to load and
quick to shoot, even from the
back of a galloping horse. It wa:
accurate at long range, too

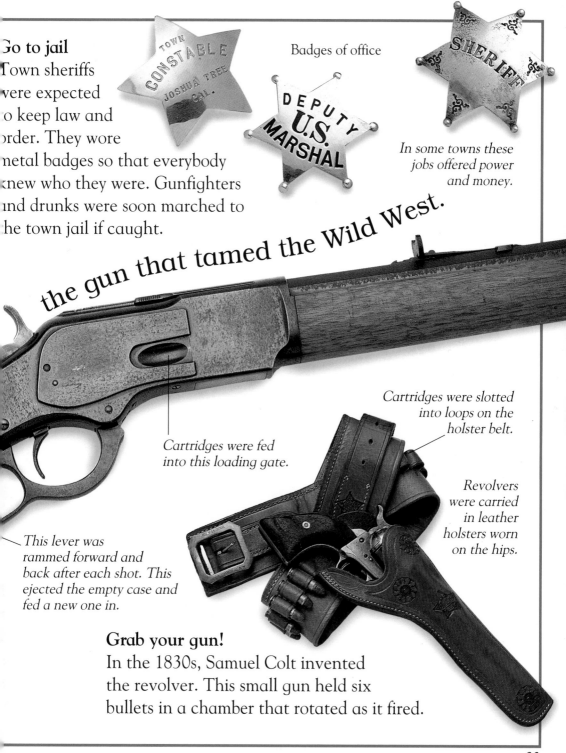

Go to jail

Town sheriffs were expected to keep law and order. They wore metal badges so that everybody knew who they were. Gunfighters and drunks were soon marched to the town jail if caught.

Badges of office

In some towns these jobs offered power and money.

the gun that tamed the Wild West.

Cartridges were fed into this loading gate.

Cartridges were slotted into loops on the holster belt.

Revolvers were carried in leather holsters worn on the hips.

This lever was rammed forward and back after each shot. This ejected the empty case and fed a new one in.

Grab your gun!

In the 1830s, Samuel Colt invented the revolver. This small gun held six bullets in a chamber that rotated as it fired.

Cowboys

Films often portray cowboys as glamorous characters. But trail drives were hard work.

All work and no play
Cowboys drove cattle herds north to meet trains going east. Some of these herds were over a mile long and contained up to 2,500 cows!

1850s Texas saddle

A sturdy wardrobe
A cowboy's clothes had to be strong, and they had to protect him from the sun and wind, and from scratches. On top of long-lasting woolen pants, he wore stiff leather chaps in case he had to chase a stray cow through thorny bushes.

Chaps

Whoa there!

It took little to frighten a herd of cattle into stampeding, but it was hard to stop them. The cowboys had to gallop ahead and force the leading cattle back in tighter and tighter circles.

Driving a huge herd of cattle was tough work.

Saddle blanket

Metal hoops supported a canvas cover.

Meals on wheels

Herding was hungry work, and a cook was employed to supply meals from a chuck wagon. A typical meal was a plate of bacon, beans, and greasy fried bread. Yum!

Ride 'em cowboy!

In 1883, a buffalo hunter called Buffalo Bill put on a Wild West show – a show packed with fast riding and skillful shooting.

Women of the West
One woman who never missed her target was Annie Oakley. Annie performed in Buffalo Bill's Wild West show as a trick-shot.

The word rode

Rodeo fun
To this day, rodeos give millions
of people a chance to see the
skills of the Wild West.

_Lariats
were made
of stiff hemp
or rawhide._

is Spanish for roundup.

_A cowboy
always aims
for the cow's
horns or legs._

Cut and chase
Catching a cow for
branding took great
skill from both the
cowboy and his horse.
Horses were specially
trained for "cutting" a
cow from its herd, and
then chasing it until
the cow was roped.

On track

In 1869, the East and West coasts of America were joined by rail. A journey that had taken months now took days.

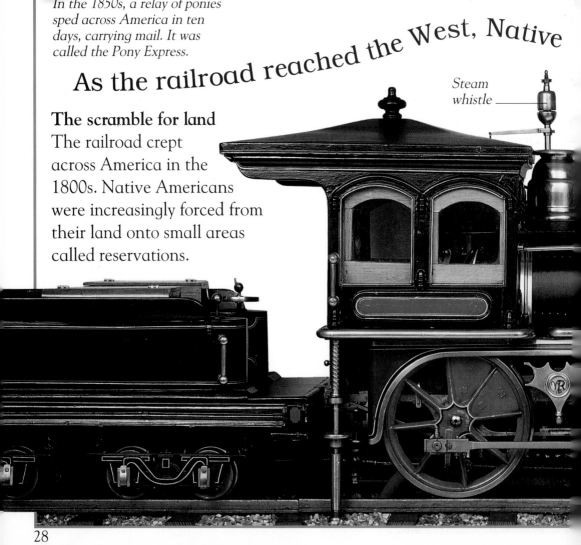

In the 1850s, a relay of ponies sped across America in ten days, carrying mail. It was called the Pony Express.

As the railroad reached the West, Native

Steam whistle

The scramble for land
The railroad crept across America in the 1800s. Native Americans were increasingly forced from their land onto small areas called reservations.

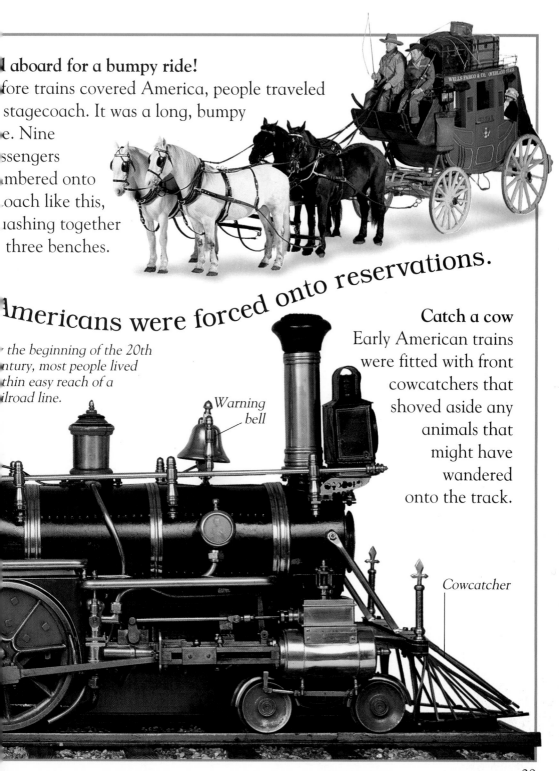

l aboard for a bumpy ride!
fore trains covered America, people traveled
stagecoach. It was a long, bumpy
e. Nine
ssengers
mbered onto
.oach like this,
uashing together
three benches.

Americans were forced onto reservations.

the beginning of the 20th
ntury, most people lived
thin easy reach of a
ilroad line.

Warning bell

Catch a cow
Early American trains
were fitted with front
cowcatchers that
shoved aside any
animals that
might have
wandered
onto the track.

Cowcatcher

29

Index

Five quick-draw questions

1) What was a cradleboard?

2) Which bird has become a national emblem?

3) When was the gold rush?

4) What was wampum?
   (a) a temporary summer home
   (b) shells
   (c) a dance
   (d) a sticky food

5) Which city was known as the "Cowboy Capital of the World"

Answers on page 32

Answers

From page 30:

1) A baby carrier
2) The bald eagle
3) 1849
4) (b) shells
5) Dodge City